Sharing A trail

Markell Sorp

MPW LLC

This trail is special, This park is Free
This place is made for you and me
And He and She and They and Them
For any person, at any whim

Not like your toys, not like your food
Parks are for joy, but for others, too

We share the trail with everyone
So on the trail let's not be dumb

There are some rules like every place
They are in place to keep you safe
And keep us all so comfortable
That we have no worries at all

Rule number one stay to the right
Yes to the right, like when we drive
This path, this trail is like a road
Walk to the left and you'll hear groans

Not only groans but close calls, too
For if you do, they'll have to move

Off their line and out of yours
But into mine, we're all off course

Predictable, what we should be!
nobody's mind can we read!

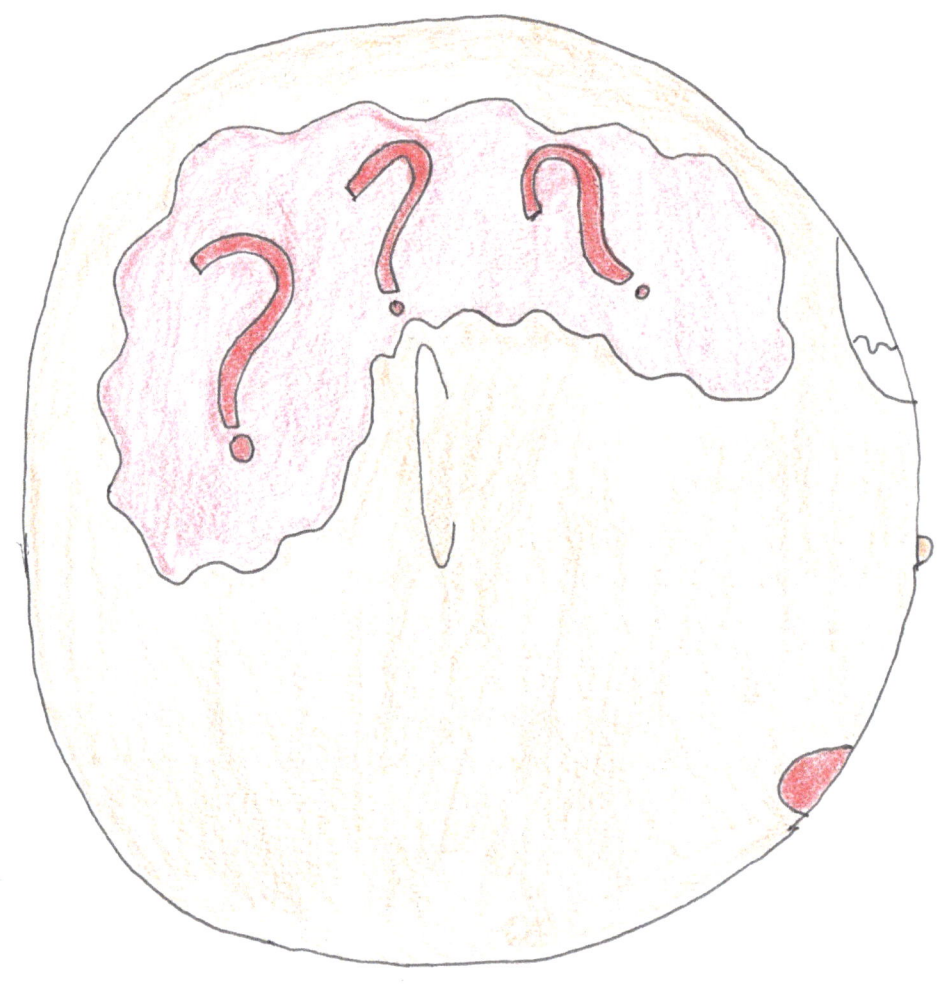

Stay to the right and keep it there
This is a place that we all share!

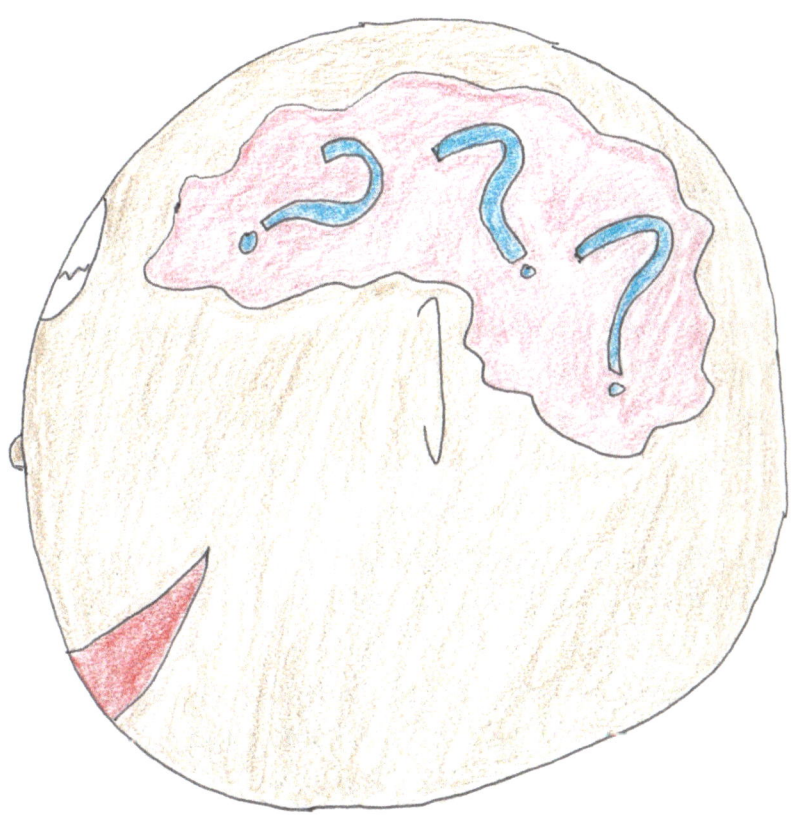

Now everyone has a different pace
A different pace in this place
So leave some space on the side
For those who run and those who ride

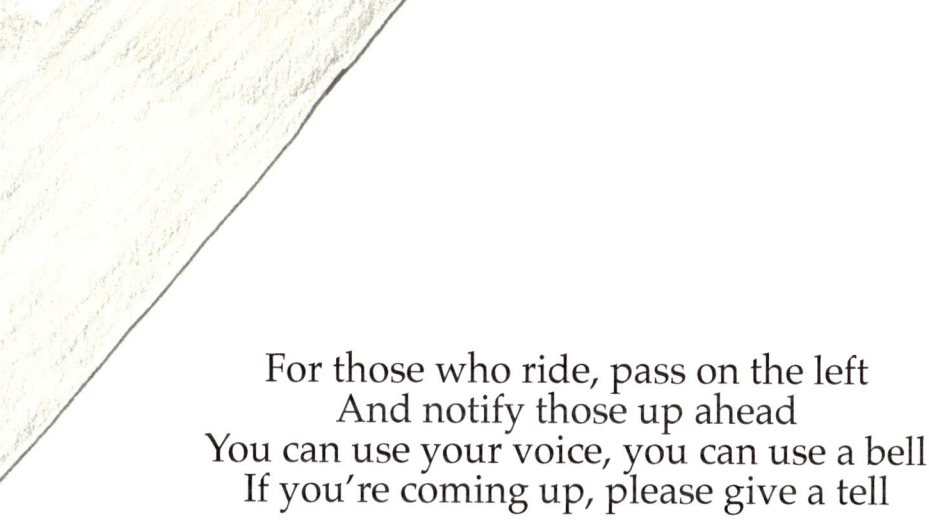

For those who ride, pass on the left
And notify those up ahead
You can use your voice, you can use a bell
If you're coming up, please give a tell

This is the rule named number two
This passing rule's for runners, too
But use your voice, if not a bell
Rule number two keeps us safe as well

Walking, running, riding with cheer
Never neglect, you must still hear
Rule number 3 keep your ears clear
At least one open when you're out here

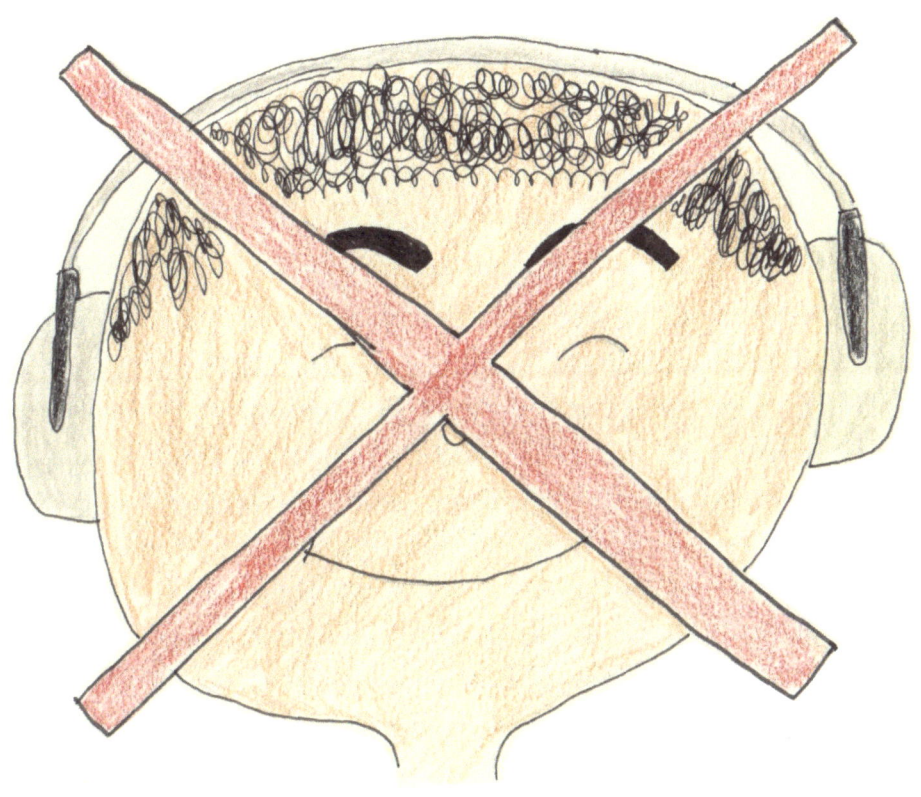

So one ear bud is perfectly fine
But two's a no, on-ear's a crime
You need to be aware in time
Emergencies and those behind

Lo

Just stay aware and be alert
It's for yourself, you won't get hurt
And others, too, you never know
Sometimes we trip or lose control

Speaking of Control, please bring a lead
Yes, for your dog, they need be leashed

For the Obedient and the well trained
The public is not for their free rein

That's number 4, it's for your pets
And all the time, clean up your mess
After your pets, after your food
Leave none behind, there's no excuse

After 5, then there's 6
Be considerate, yeah, that's it
Please be mindful, please be kind
With that in mind, we'll all be fine!

Don't want to hear what's on your phone
We're at a park, you're not at home
Enjoy your time, embrace outside
The Birds, the Bees, the Squirrels, oh my!

That's pretty much it, of course there's more
Most have some sense not to ignore
Don't vandalize do not deface
Keep this park, this trail a lovely place!

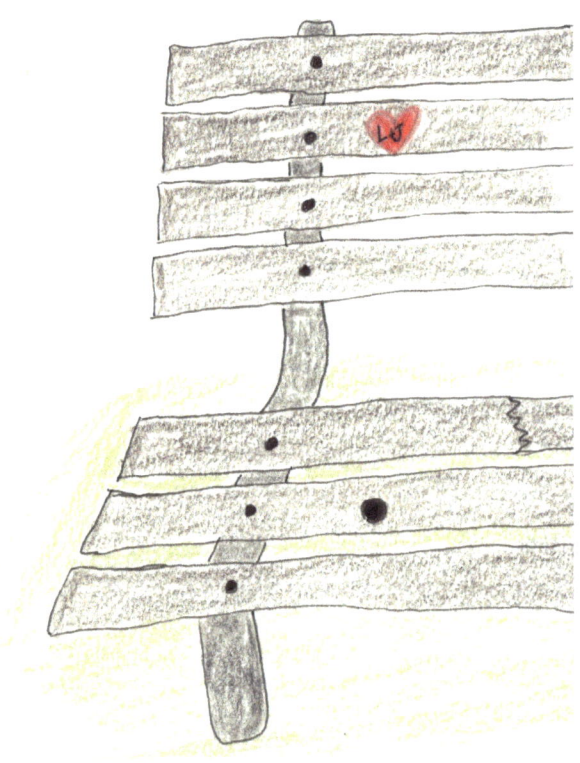

So every time we come back here
Or any park in any year
Keep this in mind, and keep this dear
We're Sharing a trail, please adhere!

www.ingramcontent.com/pod-product-compliance
Lightning Source LLC
Chambersburg PA
CBHW040901120626
46551CB00001B/113